TURANE : THE HIDDEN VILLAGE

PATRICK DEELEY

DEDALUS

DUBLIN

The Dedalus Press
24 The Heath,
Cypress Downs,
Dublin 6W
Ireland 20/9/95

ISBN 1 873790 69 4(paper)
ISBN 1 873790 70 8 (bound)

Cover design by Michael Boran

for Judy, Alan and Genevieve
and for my East Galway heartland

Acknowledgements are made to the editors of the following publications where some of these poems were first published: *Poetry Ireland Review; Toward Harmony, A Celebration for Tony O'Malley; Cúirt: The Journal; The Irish Times; Writing in the West; Cyphers; Tracks : The Snow path.*

Dedalus Press Books are represented and distributed abroad by Password, 23 New Mount St., Manchester M4 4DE.

Printed in Ireland by Colour Books Ltd.

The Dedalus Press receives financial assistance from An Chomhairle Ealaíon, The Arts Council, Ireland.

CONTENTS

DOORSTEP

Did darkness draw the rooks
to the trees,
or the rooks draw darkness?

Seven year old me
wrestled the Use of Reason
to a headlock over this,

but shortly my mother called us
for supper and a spoon
of cod liver oil

rinsed down with tea,
so we just left them there
to happen anyway –

darkness, the rooks,
in weary bits, in black scraps,
clothing the branches.

A CUT OF BREAD

Ptuh! His spit blackened
the flat emery stone
which he had taken
from above the fireplace.

But it was the pig-knife
focused my attention
as he angled its blade
for sharpening. Sound

such as rubbed paper
makes, but I kept hearing
haemoglobin, haemoglobin,
each syllable a stressed

message in my veins.
His pitying smile
played between his mother
and me. *Did anyone*

see ya comin' in?
And his mother said :
Ah Mattie, will ya lave
the poor child alone?

He yanked back my head,
exposing the small Adam's
apple to the blade.
Be Jasus they won't see

ya goin' out! This
torture led to a cut
of Mrs. Burke's homemade
bread. *Ah can't ya lave ...*

The bounty and the malice
bring me back again
to the way it was, rites
of passage and denial

colouring fun, fervour,
fear, no easy coming in
to my *haemoglobin,*
ah Mattie, be Jasus, ptuh!

SAND-QUARRY SKULL

We sat it on the big
tool-welted carpentry
workbench, turned it
round and round, slow
cranial-dome world
of caves and hillocks

a desert in our hands.
But still, but still,
the skull reminded us
of ourselves. We dreamed
ways by which a vessel
might fill, pour, be

lipped, tasted, known,
might reciprocate or
seem to, might find
the decency of a deep,
a lasting clay-break,
when its time is done.

MINDING GOAL

One consequence of being stuck
between the netless posts
during hurling practice
was to be guaranteed at least
the task and satisfaction
of hanging the sliotar out.

The others clashing and chasing,
jerseyed in various club
and county colours, dreamed
themselves glorious. You squinted
through the oblique sunlight
or pretended the shape of ease,

or crouched, or paced, depending.
A save adorned the goal
opposite, and swiftly the game
turned. Solo-specialist Joe
closed in, all wrist and speed
as he balanced the sliotar

on his hurley before swivelling
to lash it past your ear.
What kept you there? Hardly
the prospect of making a save.
And retrieval was a long walk
no-one else would take, a slash

search through lank grass.
Turane Little, Spring twilight –
the losing and the laying claim
both implicit in a sphere
of corded leather tossed up
before your face, and given air.

TONY SEES A GHOST

The big sack of flour
has fallen, and I
must lug it upright

if only because
it passes for myself,
blocking the way

of swingable space,
preventing a door.
I grip its thin cotton,

slap for purchase –
sudden powder-burst
raises the ghost

of a boy with a hurl
to my blinded face.
His knobby knees

are stained with mud
and grass, the long
loose pair of togs

he keeps pulling up
is a flour-sack
scissored and stitched.

I reel away from
the picture of health
he ambles round in.

THE LESSON OF FARROWING

The biggest bulb I had ever seen
breathed out of its goblin face
a stifling light – infra red –
on hands, on straw, on sow

stretched grumbling in her crate.
The first piglet came. I clutched it,
small firm hot and bothered
parcel. My scissors snipped

the pulsing umbilical. Steam ghosts
rose as I held the piglet close
to that ring-crusted mother snout
and heard her grunt become

a pig laugh, a tender greeting.
My heart deliciously wobbled,
making the stench of birthing easy
to forgive. She littered twelve

in all under the bulb's crimson.
I dugged each. Buckets and trough
took her place. The young rooted
for bliss and other nutrients

until we ringed their noses
with a double-S pincers. I learned
the lesson of farrowing soon enough –
all of the bonhams except one

creeled in the fat of autumn,
this last kept, fill for a wooden
barrel, to be flitched and eaten.
Was it me left the door unlatched,

now he had skedaddled
beyond the Callows, breasting Dwyer's
stream, free-range and on his way
at the last reported sighting?

Mattie Burke organised a posse,
and they roped the pig in a shamble
of bulrushes. His pitched scream
was a woeful prescience

of the dunted gash in his throat
to come. And I, for my sin,
would be given the job of garnering
his blood in a white enamel basin.

GIFT

for Tom O'Malley

A *fountain* pen. The word
doubled the actual gift.
I conjured the splash
and tinkle of water-plumes,

piazza sun juggling
a glitter of half-crowns,
florins and shillings
among them all year round.

But the nearest I'd come
to Rome was our local church,
its marble altar, Latin
Mass, and in the porch

a recurrence of the word –
now curtailed to *font*,
or so I argued,
because it wouldn't splash.

My pen could do that,
jetting its own blue colour
at a mortal friend across
the desk if I lifted a lever,

sometimes even blobbing
headlines I'd made clear.
It turned to second nature
in my left hand. All

discovery thought to spark
it off. A frog's croak
the sound by which it drank.
A devil's coach-horse

gut. A smooth rhizome
its feel and shape. A wasp
on wood its golden nib,
gently scraping the page.

PAKIE'S FREE

It's a damnable thing, Jeemie,
my first uncle says,
and Jeemie, who's heard this
lamentation since Athenry,

exhales a *Jez be ta Christ.*
Turloughmore have won the county,
and we're heading home
bet, in my first uncle's

rickety vehicle. He changes
gear, rocking indulgently
back and forth. A consolation
I smile at behind his head,

who have my own healing memory –
sliotar a soaring stillness
that begins to compose me
soon as it leaves Pakie's hurley.

A metamorphic flight, lark
elongating into playful stoat
which twists downwards
into eel, then kingfisher's

dipping and it's a salmon
stranded in the net that shakes
and shakes, spider trampolining,
cheerdom around me risen.

LANGUAGES

for Simon and Vincent

Whirr! The sawmill blade
blurs in response
to a burst of smoke
from the revved
tractor's exhaust pipe.

I sit in the tin seat,
watching the distended 8
of the leather belt
smoothly recycling itself
between pulleys.

You align the ash log
for splitting, then propel
the rollered twin-plank
on which it rests
forward, nearer, along.

Skirr! Skaarm! Sklup!
The touch, the cleaving,
uncaptureable
in any consonants or
vowels of mine,

the wood's silent language
your particular concern.
I sit for hours,
raising and lowering
the tractor's voice.

It stutters or races,
depending on what you ask
the saw to do.
The whole village hears
our industry's vocabulary.

Heads are shaking
in benign disapproval.
O let them at it,
they'll get tired yet.
And when we finally quit,

the silence bewilders.
Carry the planks indoors
to the workshop
and stack them, tome after
tome, on its rafters.

GRANDFATHER

His hay spirit
festers beside a silage pit.
He hears trespass –
electric fence,
gas-banger scarecrow.
He puzzles what the drills
grow. Requests
an almanac of fair days
to be said by. And,
field after field, tackles
the vanished horse.

FRIENDS

Me and PJ. PJ and me.
Whichever way I put it
sounded good. A score

of years approximated
to the size of us. Ran,
raided, hurled, fought –

all one. Slugged
the altar wine behind
Father Doran's back,

knocked the heads
off tulips parading
along by Teacher's wall.

Bathed in Dwyer's Spring
which half the village
drew on for drinking.

Adventured. Friends
far as mortality went.
Until the May evening

in Turane Little
when a tinker lad
stood on the sideline

watching us hurlers
train. *Get rid of 'im,*
our reffing mentor barked

in my direction. I gaped
at the watery eyes
and nose, the snotted

sleeve, the sawn-off
wellingtons banding black
chafe-marks across

his spindly shanks,
and changed my mind.
PJ said I was chicken.

Just watch this!
He waded in with hurley
flailing, battered

that tinker lad down.
They're the same
as animals, he shrugged,

when someone chided him
about doing the dirt.
But I knew it'd never be

PJ and me, me and PJ,
again. Not that I was
better than him,

merely the recognition
of my own soft spot,
open to the world's hurt.

JOAN, AGED EIGHT AND A HALF

She can run not quite fast
as the wind or a horse,
the black collie or even
a pig on the loose, but faster
far than any donkey derby.

Earwigs are her latest hobby.
Not much about them
she doesn't know.
Cross her heart, hope to die,
they hatch and nestle

their young, and moonlight
makes them fly. She vows
they'll hibernate
in the cotton-lined hollows
of old *Queen Anne's Lace*.

Someone should tell her
that such things don't always
have to happen just so.
That certain things never.
But then, who would think to?

PURPLE FACE

Suddenly again we were boys,
unable to swear or smoke
our few measly Silk-Cut butts,

because he had dismounted
there by the drystone wall
on which we sat. Brendan Kane,

upright citizen of Turane.
If our fathers heard tell ...
Except that now his eyes

were gazing in at the girls,
who whirled their circle
in the hollow of the lios.

Whoosha, Whoosha, all fall down.
He was holding the push-bike
slightly away from him

and stroking its bony saddle.
Oddly, the gesture reminded
of how my mother coaxed

big sister's long-maned head
at bedtime towards the comb.
Nice evenin'. He didn't

acknowledge as we moved off,
leaving the girls to run
themselves and their games.

Each in the end slept sound
at home. Except for Joan,
whom Brendan Kane followed,

harmed. Mother's heart-scald,
child's own pain. Brendan Kane
skulked still. A hot kettle

caught him flush. Ever after,
he wore the purple face. It
branded him. It was a sign.

JOAN, AGED NINE

This is not a nice place.
Friends aren't friends.
Smiles could mean anything.
Who hides in the bushes?
People can hurt you.
Earwigs have sharp pincers.
This is not a nice place.
People aren't friends.
Earwigs hide in the bushes.
Smiles could mean pincers.

THE CRUCIFIXION OF TOMMY JOE

Tommy Joe, telling himself,
telling us, he's *sartin*-sure
that his *yows* will lamb,
his *wainlens* fatten, his *meddas*
ripen, all in *nakure's* time.

Tommy Joe, venturing out
and back in his big buff coat,
who never bothered at all
with the *wimmin*, whose house
might be empty without him, so.

Tommy Joe, aged fifty nine,
owing a pound to no-one
and himself not being owed,
moochingly loosening a button
to piss on the frosty road.

Tommy Joe, asking no more
than the Tribune of a Thursday,
the quiet pint nightly, faithfully
follying the hurlers though they
wouldn't puck shite off a door.

Tommy Joe, climbing the gate
to his yard undiscouraged
when foot slips, chain-wrapped
top spar snags, flinging him
headlong over, one ankle wedged.

Tommy Joe, losing his hat
to the ice-mud just under his head,
cursing, struggling, pleading,
gasping his last at a world
all gone from the way God made.

Tommy Joe, poor crucified,
whom morning will find
limp on the gate-web of iron,
his buff coat's unfurled linings
resembling flithered moth-wings.

Tommy Joe, with his back turned
to all he owned, shocking us
the news that there's no telling
what can happen when natural
justice is not your friend.

DISLOCATOR

for Ena and Bridie

Blue-black summer dusk
hides the way to Aughty hill,
but here, blistered tar
crimped into hard texts,
foretells a stone-bruise
that awaits me still,
a bumped toe bound to bleed
before I'm shod again
for September and school.

I have turned my back
to Turane Cross, the proud
petrol moon of big Mex
aloft on a crooked stem,
the fresh pan-loaf smell
of Tony's grocery shop,
where he fidgets and shakes
and can't get his hands
to work the keyed-up till.

Amn't I – the dislocator –
lucky next to him? Twice
put myself out since April,
twice the bone-setter's
pushed me back in to mend.
Pain can win servants –
go, come, go, tickle-itch
my healing – but rerun
a wonder and it's lessened :

now with sympathy slack
I'm off on a *frake* again.
Shadows rag the ditches,
sudden start of something
there, what is supernature
if not myself enthralled
by the natural, or does
a pooka's scald of piss
really flither the briar?

O, O, O, pipe the cables,
taking a short-cut across
where the road bends,
and transformer's the tall
pitched pole, hoisting
above me a portentous can,
transformer's the box
conjuring behind curtains
in Mrs. Broderick's kitchen

a tale of how the west
is won. I want to laugh –
dislocator doesn't know to cry –
at the lost befuddlement
of *walking sod*, the banshee's
broken prophecy, and laugh
again the sad sad *seanchai*,
backing out from all ye
'lectrocuted ghosts, goodbye.

Further it's the hurlers
milling in the lamps of cars,
sliotar's thud agin' a shin,
mind that leg – don't spare
the timber, creases springing
to my cheeks, *pull, Josie,*
pull, keep 'er on the carpet,
and I plant myself there,
flexing for a swing

who am declining instead
past the jagged grotto
of blue Mary Virgin
which two bats are describing,
past the gouged windows
of big draughty chapel,
the stain-glass patterns
crowning Patrick, Bridget,
Jesus in his thorning.

The oak door never closes,
and maybe Leena's within,
worrying her worn decades
down to the last stone,
maybe *Lodger* Glynn –
whom Teacher pronounces
one of life's true orphans –
is up to his bedevilment,
fumbling at the organ.

Out comes Father Doran,
whose well-fed shiny head
is considered by some
to be knowledgeable, who has
the power, unspecified
but dangerous, whom Mikie Bryan
bedads is livened more
by horses and farm-talk
than by notions of heaven.

Salute him, yes Father,
benediction, Sunday I'll be
thuribling the incense,
but meantime on a stone
two spiders are fencing
for a single silken string,
and it's Mikie Bryan's contention
that Big Ned who owns
the land doesn't own them,

that none of us owns –
not me my all-American
superhero comic magazines
on whom my brother's preying,
not our sister the mouth organ
containing sixteen reeds,
though such cadence she blows
makes us feel she owns,
not the Master his insults

nor Teacher the Lake District,
not the lambs their short runs,
the bull his long horns –
none of us owning what we use,
but now these path-stones
chat about my feet,
and self-abandon's
the message each moth
wants to bring to light.

This place dreamed us all,
path-stones to the house,
black stairs of the cypresses
inclined by breeze, spread,
ascended into blue
dusk, into summer darkness,
my turn now, make the most,
you'll be here only a while,
dreaming all this place.

TONY SELLING SWEETS

This thing grips and shakes me
harder now. I work to make a day.

The children
crowd in after school,

pushing their bits of change.
Word of my giving's

mouth to mouth.
So many bull's-eyes

stuck in the can I have a job
hacking them loose with the scoop.

And when I spill it
sideways – slur of brokenness.

There's a rare one
hooped with red and purple stripes

they ask for a lot.
I indulge them,

they take advantage.
There's a rare one

locked inside
I can't get at.

TRESPASS

Syl Kelly's young ram
is busy tipping ewes.
Scarcely a week let out
to them, and already six
wear the raddle's rub
on their hindquarters.

Two fields further,
William Daly's old ram
is restless, alone.
The musk of rutting rides
across on the breeze:
instinct empowers him

to knock down fences
whose slack credentials
have gone untested
for years. Confrontation
is a butting together
of heads, a dunting nod

in the direction
of kingdom without border
that repeats, repeats,
until Syl Kelly's ram
staggers, falls, sideways,
dead. There will be war.

LEENA ALONE

I was well off and didn't
know it, my rheumatics
quiet for the summer, only
the corncrake keeping me

awake nights. I always
took a knock at the door
for insult. Just turn
the handle, walk straight

in, bring me blessing.
There was a key you'd call
communal – I never
locked a door in my life,

far as I saw, neither
did anyone. Able-bodied
again, I cycled to Gurty,
got the few groceries.

Butter vouchers filled
my churn. I let the meadow,
kept a clocker hen.
Church devotions dusted

my knee; I had right-
of-way through darkness.
The late-callers wore
mummer masks. Whooped

a hullabaloo around me;
I was lifted and shaken.
Where's yer stash?
My mattress gutted with

their knives, my dresser
smashed. *Where's yer stash?*
The sharp years flash
across – I forget myself.

What am I now, looked at
in the glass? A face
all twitched by thin
white stitches of scars.

It's falling dark. My key
slots the lock. I hear
a reaper-and-binder working
late, but no corncrake.

CALLOWS

caladh : river meadow

No house could be built in the marshland
known as Callows, no porch-light
shine there, any night ever.

Old men umpired the space race
between *'Merica and them Rooshians,*
but to me the place of quagmires

was frontier enough. The only television
that could hold my eyes for long
was the window of my bedroom.

I'd watch while darkness drowned
the beyond, all flaggards, rushes, rivers,
one, and sometimes at a point

which promised nothing, will-o-'the-wisp
showed – waif betwixt wet fences,
he dipped, then he rose. My hands

would wipe, re-wipe the misted glass:
I'd sit and stare, ask, answer, ask.
No house be built, no porch-light

shine ... Tynagh Mine brought new fever
home, a hive of brightness
breaching the horizon. Callows still

survived – out-back escape where vixen
shifted, curlew enquired, and spider
hooked her hat to a rush-stalk.

But whoever could eat stone miles
into the earth, could drink
a *swally hole*. And that's what happened.

A STUDY IN JUTTINGS

for Jim and Ruth

Looking tonight at Gogol's
old man in an overcoat
depicted by Yuri Norstein
in flick-fade animation,

I see again Mikie Bryan,
dweller, unless he be dream,
in a black-thatch hovel
draughty as bedamned.

It's late. The cardplayers
have gone, leaving him alone
with his drowsy crickets
and a red hen which roosts

on his bed's back rail.
I hear the incessant wind
blowing through to him,
as to Norstein's citizen.

And though no avid clerk,
meticulously scribing
what the world-made-office
has done or left undone,

Mikie is a conscience, still,
stirred by beseechment
of the dead and the living
in a storm. He untwines

the day's newspapers, neatly
batched. Wrestles one,
another, open, and leaning
from the hob, relaunders

both flat. His head tilts
bird-quick, sizing up truth
in its various casts;
his sudden finger stabs.

A panicky candle-flame
on the bare wood before him
throws shadows that bounce,
then momentarily serene

ascends to full height,
cancelling shadows out.
Its perpetual poor light
works the long countenance

to a study in juttings.
He hesitates. He asserts.
Rhodesia, Congo, bother him
nights. He says names will

change, lines will shift
whole tracts of actual land.
He says the human heart
can be held in a hand

and still go on beating.
The cardplayers humour him,
yet homeward I hear them
scoff: *Rhodesia? Congo?*

That's a pagan for ya –
he makes good poitin though.
Misrepresentations will
never end. He told me so.

MIKIE BRYAN'S PUZZLEMENT

There are conflictings in
and among all creaturelings,
from most minuscule
amoeba or *protozuun*
to the machinations of men.
By times a black blinkers
slips down over my mind
and I can only discern
the wolf behind my meek
dog's eyes, the hawk abiding
in my little hen's beak,
the flowers as wretched.
And I wonder why ever humus
bothered espousing thought.

ELLIE AND THE YANK

His pulse is quicker than ours.
He sits as if there's sand
under his arse. The children
call him Showy Socks. He'll talk
travel till the cows come home,
then some! 'Frisco, L.A.,
Honolulu, New York. They're all
towns to him. Am I supposed
to be impressed? Furthest
I've gone is Dublin, the hills
of Wicklow beyond. I.C.A. outing
once. Thought each minute
an hour but there's no telling
him that. Another whiskey shot.
He might take a trip across
to see Mikie Bryan later. Always
enjoyed the old boy's style
of chat. Name-droppers both!
Goddammit Ellie, he says, *don'cha*
ever get crazy lookin' out
at those pain-in-the-ass bushes?
There'll be ease when he goes.

THE BIRTH OF TIM

Often I've assisted
calving cow, dropping *yow*,
but would not be
at Ellie's birthings,

always quick when directed
towards the delivery.
It's the woman's miracle,
I'd say quietly

after she collared me –
what use a man
unless he's medical,
what use even then

next to midwife or nurse?
Three children all born
healthy, never
did one of them raise

the fault against me –
so I romanced Ellie, joking
but implying also
I give them the evenings

for a childhood
between my other two.
You'll be staying this
time, she shouted,

meaning for Tim. And I saw
the sagacious emergence
of him, head and
oxters and long limbs –

an astronaut floated,
another pocketed the moon;
well, happier me : I
cried, so Tim, then Ellie.

ELLIE TELLS A GOOD ONE

for Mary Deeley

I was making bread at the time.
Looked out over Tim's head
at the blooming blackthorns
beyond the window, and thought

of a wedding. Maybe the flour
powdering by accident
the bump my apron couldn't hide,
drew down his eyes. But

so I stood, glugging basin
of buttermilk-dough together,
when he started pointing
and flurrying the questions.

How did that get ... ? Where did
he come from? Was I baking
a new sister? And him only four!
Likely his brats of brothers

have been pumping him up
to this touflish. *Portiuncula,*
I said, tamping the cake flat,
then reached for the knife

and cut a Sign of the Cross.
You were born in Portiuncula.
I turned towards the range
and opened it. Smelled

the blast of oven-heat. *Da-da*
puts his feet in there.
A huff of my shoulders raised
the gleeful merchant's laugh.

I smiled, picturing his father
tipped back nightly in the chair,
legs sprawled so careless
that some night'll unbalance

entire. Still, he's fond
of warming himself for the bed!
Tim pinched a morsel of dough
and tasted. *Sodaish,* he said.

CONVERSATION PIECE

When Tim told the house
that Teacher told him
and the rest of her pupils
that she is *unashamedly*
romantic, and when Tim
explained what it meant,
Ellie said she might
need to be – married
to that brute of a Master.
And Ellie's husband said
he could never respect
a man whose scholars
were afraid of their lives
of him. And Tim's brother
Jimmy said that a brown
cloud of porter-fumes
follows the Master round
the classroom some days.
And Tim said that Teacher
wears lilac perfume.
And Ellie said that maybe
the Master and Teacher
were content together
and it was up to no-one
but themselves to judge,
and that regardless
they got great results
between them. And Ellie's
husband said porter
and perfume, some blend.

TONY'S FUNERAL

Maybe the remembrance
of push-penny games
played across a counter
gone glossy with use,

will circulate a smile
around Tony's funeral –
stay a while and chat,
though the day's wet,

the plastic bouquets
drip, drip, depressing,
and lips are saying
a merciful release.

Maybe his magnificent
way of cursing, *God
blast the heap of ye
into a scarlet inferno,*

when he saw us approach,
will warm our stand
against the movements
we are and must make

now – too quick, Tony,
the words waste us up,
the nods and shakes
by which we all must go.

BODIES

The mound is always there,
a shoulder for childhood
to cry on, a hospital bed,
a frogleap, a footstool.

Bodies do not otherwise
matter much, my own, hers,
meant only for tumbling
together in a wrestle

of limbs, for crushing
fat dandelions against –
fingers to flesh to cries
of *piss in the bed, you're*

pissybeds! But now
she's grown particular
about distances, smirking
into her delicate fist

at games I propose. Some
hauteur overtakes her
and she doesn't even know
I'm up against the mound,

watching her skinny-dip
in the stream beyond.
Her particular distance,
the clay-coloured rounds

that ream her movements,
new moons that shape
her body's difference,
make my watching avid:

she is hill, I the stoppered
stream. So pressed,
the strange hot spate
of myself finds a cleft

in the mound, wanting release
forever from *mother,*
father, nurse, doctor, all
the compromise of childhood.

CONFIRMATION DAY

I'm one inch taller than Magdalena,
touching shoulders tell me this,
we will, we will, we will be soldiers
of Christ, here in the front row
standing together, hereafter
in a photo, go on, risk a glance,
one slight tilt of your head, one small
smile be towards me who am full
with devotion for your dimple –
mud-gold moves in Dwyer's stream,
soon the tadpole's confirmed amphibian;
stir your white veil, so still,
so still, one inch of tallness tells
we sleep, my Magdalena from Turane.

THE ROAD *LORG*

The tar road is
anyone's, I'm
below the head
of a blind boreen,

the clay path's
for cattle,
you can muck it
just the same,

these prints
aren't vixen's,
here's where
the rabbit runs,

step-up stile's
a good invention,
Old John he
does be leppin'

with a bucket
of mash, a dash
of calf-nut meal,
days a splash

of cold spring,
but the road
beyond Mikie's
is so lonesome

yourself loudens,
the waste road
cutting a bog
no-one will burn,

the slippery road
falling down
along its sides
and the middle

fit for joulting
a tongue-load
of lozengers,
my lumpy words –

well, hold on
now an' we'll see
do you know
what you're at –

I'm going under
a low bridge's
broken back,
then up over

a winded log,
ways I must travel
if I take
the road *Lorg*.

Note: *Lorg*, from the Irish 'ar lorg' – seeking.

OLD JOHN

Turf-heap and hay-pike
aren't where he
dreams them, who could
lilt just lately

sod's worth, saving
behind each *gabháil.*
Now he's misplaced
even the well,

misplaced it, Old John,
and gone romancing
back seventy summers
to the dancing

asterisk of a lit fuse,
the sweating keg
in a nook, the cold
clear swig

come of such crack,
water's plain truth –
arra himself
hollow with the drooth,

certain that someplace
a liquid coin
stares up, is tunnelled
long way down.

Note: *gabháil* – armful

BIG NED'S GUEST

A man can't live
on the wind. This
is a bright remark.
I feed him stir-about
after he proves
unafraid of work.

Mucks out a byre
or some such – oh,
strong as an ox
in those days, less
stooped, head full
of wiry red locks.

A man can't live
forninst a bush.
Untangling this,
I get him to shake
out his pockets.
A pipe. And matches.

Satisfied he's safe,
I bid him sleep
in the hayshed
and leave him to it,
certain he'll go
the morning road.

It looks to be true
a man can't live
in the way he says.
I work him fairly
up until April
or May, May it is,

then he absconds
for the blackthorned
breezes of summer.
Pipe and matches
remain. And an ironic
nickname. *Lodger.*

LODGER'S HIGH

Sunlight whiskers me,
cricked at the foot
of a big leafy tree.

Road finds me out,
warping with hunger
south by Cappy Cross.

Woman of the house
butters me a slice:
dog begrudges this.

Grey *cuileog* shites,
pulls a body-hair,
wipes his bitty arse.

I rub an' I scratch,
locate coinage
in my tattered fork.

Night settles down,
sups a few stars
from the noggin I sky.

Moon fills my mouth,
I hail a game bush
riding the ring-fort.

Last log ignorantly
clicks to itself,
thorny sparks fly.

Scraw of soft grass
plumps slack up
the size it should be.

TYNAGH MINE; THE LEAVINGS

1.

On my dying oath it is
our local prairie,
and little enough
to look at when we
finally get landed,
this shook-looking stretch
of thraneen grasses,
nor hair nor hide
amongst them, only
the thin wind filing
away, famishment,
I'd say, an eternity
of it, on the level.

2.

Slag-grey acres done,
this rustwater pool's
such a beguiling
beauty you incline
your eye to hers –
she's curative, she's
a spa, she's the scrumpy
of the western world,
she's all the robin
redbreasts you ever saw
warming a winter sill,
she's a Galway Bay sunset
come to molly-coddle.

MARIGOLD

for Michael Nolan

Lorg is far away
as ever, but look
at me, a man

still embarked
on vagary, stooped
to the panning

stream for a flick
of minnow.
Grassbank bounce,

the harvest frog
happens now.
Withering sedge

and marigold
in water are reamed
by skit beetles.

My stock-taking
fingers trace
a washboard brow,

my wet kneel
creaks its cold.
I rise to go,

no more the hop
skip and jump
that propelled me

once, rather
a measured pace,
longhand's

earned headway
over heart-stitch
and mirage.

STONES

I am out clamping stones,
making the same slow
precise moves my ancestors
made. And their talk
is sunlight in the gaps,
their mottled hands
specks of lichen and dust
impossible to shake off,
their only monuments
walls, passed down, handed
on, their very bones
my own after a fashion.

SCAPEGOAT

Go 'way down that bog
a dark spit below heather,
go sleán yourself
a fire for next winter.

So I draw the worn body
out afresh, so I take
its creaking limbs
to task, but little differ

all my labours make
to Gallagh Man –
he's skid-marking
the floor of an iron age,

he's danced by the neck
in a halter. Ah poor
Gallagh Man, the donkey
hang of his dangler,

whatever harm he done,
look sideways on 'im –
still a scapegoat
staked to keep his pagan

soul from flying,
and the slept flesh turns
up here, cradling
my opne-handed entreaty.

PARISH PUMP

With rusted snout
and tail not touching
the ground, this

hardy little dinosaur
is going nowhere
except backwards

to media interpretations
of ourselves
as rednecks stooping

to rinse out hayseeds
after sweaty days
spent saving meadows

which naturally lead
to grassroots growing
on a stone pedestal,

and capping us all,
the yoke itself
sports a báinín

or a class of smock-tops
such as the labourers
took to wearing

once upon a time,
yet surely this
is the spout of hickdom

where we convene
after Mass on Sundays
to work backhanders

off them we elected,
to make marriages
for our sons and daughters,

to burn the news
stuck in our craws –
but you might do better

asking the cows
that drink its water
for their opinions.

OLL 'THE CATCHER'

1

A funeral's good,
a wedding special,
a hurling match
or a mart will do,
a pub that's crowded
worth the expense
if there's an election.

2

We shake hands.
I tell you my name.
You tell me yours.
We're fast friends.
You don't forget
my name. I don't
forget anyone's.

3

You ask me to do
a good turn for you.
(I bless the red-tape
hearts of bureaucrats!)
When your entitlement
comes through, you
give me the credit.

4

Off the record, mind,
Ireland's a fecky
little ball of oddments
trying to outfloat
the westerly currents.
And her politicians?
Patchwork patriots.

COWDUNG

When *watch out!* can't
step you over or around,
but into it, just let

the word *scuther* float.
Head this way again
after rain has dabbled,

breeze and sunshine
baked, after the brazen
yellow dungfly's flown.

There is scattered now
nature's good mould –
slowly crumbling back

into clay. And greenest
grasses imaginable,
freshly begun to shoot.

OLIVER J. MARTIN,
PROMOTER, 1966

I rise up from
the ranks of wallflowers
and shy countrymen,
to entice among
besuited showbands
rolling off covers
of sentimental songs.

I hear the jingle
of spare shillings
sifted in trousers
anxious to get going
out on a good time,
grease for the loins,
a bit of a dance.

I open my hands
to slacken the grip
of obdurate clergymen,
piously promise
percentages to roof
church and residential.
But there's no place

until I settle
into the shodding
of a big ignorant field,
yoke up canvas
fly-by-night beading
of bulbs to the six-pole.
Great entertainment

outside and in,
oh Ireland swings
for some, and there's
others singing
romance can't swing
her at all – but
begod now I'm shining.

OLIVER MARTIN, MEP

Turane? No, I don't
return half often enough.
And now Strasbourg,
these desked documents,
agendas, committees,
keep me: I'm tick-tacking

the emergent Europe.
A strong voice matters
here, you could call me
huxter, horse-trader,
a broker, a lobbyist even,
meanings need change

only in their magnitude –
well, that's as maybe,
for I still remember
hock-and-fetlock days,
mouth of every nag deal
pulled back to reveal

a gapped grin at October
Fair. And the father,
a grazer of Long Acre,
beating down Cheap Jack
to gather me my first
suit off the rack. It

was a start. Whereafter
I got into marquees,
until that storm broke.
Football stood to me,
an All-Ireland leg up
by which I was elected.

My new residence sits
above Loughrea's *speckled
lake of legends*. I mean
to push a boat out
there in trout season
with my German friends.

LODGER DITCHED

Haven't you a tongue
in your head? Can't
you ask? Home truths

of the hard fathers
hit at me here, lost.
A clip on the ear

from a flying twig
is good enough
to knock some sense

when it storms.
Mea culpa, mea culpa,
breasting the rain.

Neither wind nor rain
nor roadside grass
can wash clean

this turnip I munch,
tasting cut lip
and clay moustache.

DUSKUS

My father swings a phrase
across the hollow :
duskus is falling –
but I keep making hay.

The Lios field's plotted
already, only this
rakeable weave
of rye-grass and rushes

down in Old Tillage
remains. Mid July,
my twenty fifth birthday,
pismires fairly fly,

they take a shine
to the white shirt;
live wire bodies –
I just let them comb.

Duskus is falling,
only now do I feel it,
your story, father,
a lyric tendered

over the way. And even
if I know the ending,
tell me – what
were we beginning to say?

WOAD

I cup my hands
under the black drippage
of the *Ink Cap,*
and daub my face.

Hands shake, awed mouth
registers the loss
of a strange
yet fatherly spirit.

Weathering of days,
weeks, years. The woad's
dispersed to crevices
which deepen

where it congeals.
I show myself up
as someone else.
The mourning never heals.

COMING TO TERMS

No sense raving,
neighbours advise,
futile, futile it is
to persist in praising trees,
the beyond praise.

But I have seen
you in the act of felling
always offer praise,
even in your falling
felt you bless.

And I must fuse
this with this,
father no more, no less,
futile, futile it is
not to try to bless.

A PLANED DREAM OF WOOD

Let it endure then, endure,
for the carpenter now is done,
and resting all his future
in a mossy spot beneath
a bough, in a long *striall*
of shavings belonging to
the workshop, in the wood-air
of his still enterprise –
uncontactable there, but there
surrounded by hand-saws,
chisels and hanging augers.

THE OLD HEADSTONES

They lean. They sink down crumbling
round-shouldered. The very air
is eating them. Blithe colonies
of lichen nibble the fretted
inscriptions; but Mathias Hanrahan,
whose last words were an enquiry
as to whether or if the goose
would be cooked, Christmas Day 1861,
and Sarah Kilcoyne, mother
of fourteen, stumbling in famishment
for a canister of flour off
the neighbours, dwell among us still,
dwell, are verifiable, beloved
morsels in the mouth of race memory.

CANADA

He came back grey
as a badger, otherwise
the same Syl Kelly.

Mad for farming,
delighted in pulling
a calf or doing a pick.

And how was Canada,
Syl? *Temporary.*
That's all the news

he brought from
twenty winters away.
So weren't we

strange, anticipating
airs! He'd have
no meas on a man

who couldn't hold
to a pint or his own
accent. Once

on a jaunt to town
he asked and I answered
poetry brought me.

Poultry? I got
an earful of nesting
coops, hen-runs

and the out-lay
on Rhode Island Reds.
But, forget geese,

turkeys would be
the coming Christmas.
All poet-notions

plucked, pin-feathered,
bougáned! Land
he hungered for,

land he understood.
Outbid Big Ned
for Leena's meadow,

coaxed stray fields
in minding Old John.
The pastoral jigsaw

his for an Irish mile;
Canada learned him –
an able dealer, Syl.

TURLOUGH

He hesitates, then goes
out past the rusked
edge, underfoot snap
of thin dry white ice –

further, deeper, Tim,
beyond the last trace
of sallow grass-tufts,
until even the rushes

are barely tall enough,
and his picked steps
saunter into a slide
that takes him centre

of the frozen turlough.
If he looks down now,
he'll see a youth
carelessly stretched,

shirt-sleeves puckered
up, one arm visored
across the forehead
of a summer's evening,

all exams completed,
the waiting begun,
two temporary things –
himself, his situation.

TRAVELOGUE

Considerations of a Sunday,
Meadow Court disco, Kiltormer
céilí, long haul to Seapoint,
but Tim's doing a line
with a girl from Ballymacward,
and that's where he'll go.

Picking up passengers
along the way. And they chorus
behind him, you're fierce
obligin', Tim, the smirking
shower of blaggards, any chance
of a lift home? That's if

we don't shift, Tim, I feel
the sap risin' tonight,
there's an angel from th' Mercy
prayin' over me, I've a horn
that would pike a donkey
out of a boghole in Gleann!

Tim just smiles offended,
cue three mule-brays, an' that
will do now, it ain't
safe at all sittin' next
nor near ya! Ballymac. Hah!
The racked hair and the shone

shoe, the clatter of pool and
the shandy swallow. He'll drop
them in it, he'll pull up
outside her father's farmhouse,
she'll emerge, all smiles,
through a porchlit interval.

AN EXILE RETURNS

Seven years scattered,
still the familiar
gravel under my shoes.

Seven years the batter,
lone pine windbreak
bending and scraping –

the way I remember Mam
beyond this gable.
Seven years ganged up,

and the costly suit
pretends a plenitude
of earnings. Porch

window-latch is loose,
I can admit myself
to the sleeping house.

Dog, the dead hours
will make a difference,
but you lick my face.

ELLIE AND THE YEARS

Magdalena, my eldest,
wants her arse kicked
for leaving this parlour
the way a pig eats.

In her wake the vanity
things lie scattered –
sculpting mousse, lavender
neck lotion, a perfume

called *Forever*. More
elaborate you won't get
than our Magdalena!
But then she's heedless

as the dead hairs left
behind on her comb,
the long black hairs
that changed a tomboy

into a lady, heedless
as the hairs that set
my hand back-combing now
through the years

and the touch of grey
to where I can see
in a mirror more simple,
and this ring fits me.

ELLIE'S DIM VIEW OF THE SERMON

Father Doran falls into a purple rage,
and we are detained all morning
at Second Mass. Abortion! Contraception!
Jackasses of men! Women receiving
a welt of his tongue! No wonder the aisles
start coughing, a flock-protest
in mumbles and shuffles can't hush him.

Such language! Embarrassing old people,
putting thoughts in the heads of children.
I like Father Doran better when he
paints us a picture of God the
Thoroughbred galloping through fields.
The only horse I see now is Father Doran's
nag, biting the rumps off cattle.

WIFE

He stopped talking to me –
not suddenly or because
we couldn't agree, not out of
some running grievance
unless the lack of children
became silence eventually,
but I had wept that want
more than he, I had known
the fault wasn't this body –

no tracing why he stopped,
bit by bit, by the fire
at evening when farmwork
was seen to, behind a paper
after meals or in front
of the TV, with a grunted
response to all I'd offer
he stopped, with a shrug,
a sigh, a look, and the more

taciturn he grew, the louder
my talk, until forsakenly
delph spoke, pots clanged me,
entire household shook –
and at last he began to say,
with his lips, his heart,
listening, vulnerable, back,
the years mounted behind us
no longer having their way.

OCTOBER

And when I look again,
the Virginia creeper
is sending this pebble-dash
gable of my house
up in cold damp flames;
so many turning colours
I can't find where one
ends, another begins,
or fully enumerate them
other than to say *October,*
it's October already –
and Magdalena, the saying
stills me, the act
of looking dazes my eye.

HIBERNATION

Mikie storing up his bones
along the lag weeks, edge to
edge of winter solstice,

in dreams may breathe
on a lens, a lens, a lens
of the Hubble telescope.

Oatmeal and a gulp of water
from the galvanise pail
keep his marrow making,

there's blood-sustenance
in a raw egg, but seldom
at all he'll stir out

unless to pooley or piss
under the crab-apple ditch.
And what will newspapers

be but passing glances,
world a fable he concocts,
who by crank of nature

is up till Tibb's Eve
eleven moons of the year,
burning candle-wax.

So let them connected
to the electric juice
hob-nob, bloom, beyond this

big bolster his head
barely dents, this pulled
blind, this topcoat over him.

MATTIE DIGS A GRAVE

The oul shagger's dead now,
who'll be sorry for him?
There at the Cross of Turane
pontificatin' about troubles
not his own. Described himself
as a pagan, be Jasus!
Why was he frikened of the dark
so? Refused me poitin
the once I went cardplayin',
said it would burn holes
in an illiterate's mind.
They laughed, sure they did.
Only time the nerve failed me.
I should have wrung his
scrawny fuckin' neck! Strength
enough in me bare hands
to do it, I've damaged men
for less, but say nothin'
now the oul shagger's dead.
I'll sweep the clay over him,
gratefully, when Father Doran
an' them few neighbours
are gone. I'll sweep the clay
in one mighty shovelful,
an' dance it down with a curse
of purest joy. Let him be
that book of the Master's,
an' this me very last schoolday.

MATTIE'S REBUKE

That's his version of oul sores
an' recent events, not mine or yourn.
That's his own funeral, expectin'
to bundle us wind an' limb
into a chronicle them Townies might
fun over. An' didn't the wool
grow soft on him, imaginin' we'd
welcome the attention? You! Read it
out to me. But be quick!
I'm half-whipped with the rewirin'
of Daly's house – circuits,
junction boxes, an' the safe
earthin's for loose energy. He don't
say an'thin' of that now, do he?

SALLY ROD

Host of shoots insurrecting
the moot, streamlet running
away from school. And then

this tallest sally rod occurs to me
because I have culled it
in another, before : cane-material

selected by the Master,
a stick to beat 'Rithmetic into us!
But now the leap he urged me towards

from his dry dock is more a case
of reaching hands – yours, PJ, last
spotted on an oil-rig

off the coast of Maracaibo, yours,
Shamie, still cooled by local clay –
I am snatching back childhood's clasp

in a thin-skinned, tissue-peeling
silver-green sally rod, I am swinging it
lightly before me along our road.

MONAMANDRAGH REVERIE

for Seamus and Damaris

A horse-hair mattress for me
tonight, in a big room
whose black chimneyplace holds
a bundle of kindle dropped
by nest-fired jackdaws.

Here, mid-high between
the silence-fermenting cellar
and that spirit of air
registered up next the roof,
slow beguilement of centuries –

I dream your hunted priest,
shaking wet, your look-out boy
sat at a small window,
refuge, quest, Monamandragh,
ghosts I'll never flesh,

but morning moulds my own live
lift, chopping logs, binding
jigsaw walls of drystone,
tamping scraw-roots down
in the bog of the wet parsnip.

Monamandragh : bog of the wet parsnip.

UNDER THE BRIDGE

1

Water must be
a complete
and constant caress
to fish, water
dreaming for aeons
of only itself,

until the dream
snags on something
and there's life,
cell so small,
multiple
diffusion and gel,

every organ,
all appetite,
the great paddle,
perfect dovetail
of scales
into a wet suit.

2

Climb out of there
before you catch
your death,
climb stiff
red-buttocked
up off that rock,

take silence
and the vast sky
with you along,
take the freckled
sweetness
of a rainbow trout

home to the pan,
again be struck
by the notion
that no-one should
ever miss us
when we're gone.

ENDEAVOUR'S END

Hurry home and meet
your own again.
Little daughter
is digging juice
out of a grapefruit
with her spoon,
and young son makes
old ivories bell
four clear chimes
in slow succession.
The dark is early
no matter when,
so taste, so listen,
the tang, the tune.